How and Why Science

Science
in
the
Water

How and Why Science

Science in the Water

World Book, Inc.

Chicago London Sydney Toronto

Acknowledgments

The publisher of Childcraft gratefully acknowledge the courtesy of illustrator John Sandford and the following photographers, agencies, and organizations for the illustrations in this volume. When all the illustrations for a sequence of pages are from a single source, the inclusive page numbers are given. Credits should be read from left to right, top to bottom, on their respective pages. All illustrations are the exclusive property of the publisher of Childcraft unless names are marked with an asterisk (*).

6-7 Donna Coveney, MIT News Office*
24-25 Save Our Streams from the Izaac Walton League*
26-27 Bob Daemmrich*

World Book, Inc.
525 West Monroe
Chicago, IL 60661

Editors: Sharon Nowakowski, Melissa Tucker
Art Director: Wilma Stevens
Illustrator: John Sandford
Cover Design: Susan Newman
Cover Illustration: Eileen Mueller Neill

Library of Congress Cataloging-in-Publication Data

Science in the water.
    p. cm. -- (How and why science)
    Includes index.
   Summary: Discusses the properties and uses of water and presents related experiments and activities that can be performed at home. Includes games, folklore, instructions for keeping a lab notebook, and an answer key.
    ISBN 0-7166-7112-3 (pbk.)
    1. Water--Juvenile literature. 2. Water--Experiments--Juvenile literature. [1. Water. 2. Water--Experiments. 3. Experiments.] I. World Book, Inc. II. Series.
GB662.3.S35   1998
551.46--dc21   98-15682

For information on other World Book products, call 1-800-255-1750, x2238, or visit us at our Web site at http://www.worldbook.com

Printed in Singapore

1 2 3 4 5 6 7 8 9 02 01 00 99 98

Introduction

When you think about our planet, do you picture solid ground made up of rock, sand, or soil? Many people do. But in fact, the earth is a watery world. More than 70 per cent of its surface is covered by oceans. Life on earth depends on water, so you can see how important it is to learn about **Science in the Water**.

Science helps people answer questions such as, "How do fish move through the water? How do rivers grow? How can we keep our water clean and pollution-free?"

In this book, all kinds of scientists show you how they study the world. Don't worry about not understanding unfamiliar words, they are defined in the margins. A science game and a folk tale add to the fun. The **Aha!** feature highlights surprising science facts. When you are ready to try your skills, check out the **In Your Lab** sections.

Science is not just for professional geologists or environmental scientists. Science helps all of us understand the world around us, and teaches us to protect our natural resources.

Learning from Fish

No one has ever built a ship that functions in water as well as a fish. You'd almost expect me to say that, wouldn't you? After all, I'm an ichthyologist (IHK thee AHL uh jist). That's a real tongue twister, but the word just means that I'm a scientist who studies fish.

Fish have been navigating the oceans a lot longer than humans have. And fish are very good at what they do. For example, did you know the following:

Ichthyology (IHK thee AHL uh jee) comes from a Greek word that means "fish." Ichthyology is the branch of zoology that deals with fish.

- A fish can turn in a space less than a third of its body length. A ship needs one to three times its length to make a turn!

- Many fish can reverse direction without slowing down, something no ship can do.

How do we know these fascinating facts? We know because of people like Michael and George Triantafyllou, ocean engineers who study how fish swim. They believe that studying fish can help people design better submarines—subs that might be used for things such as deep-sea research or work on offshore oil rigs.

A team led by these engineers has built a robot called "Robotuna" that mimics, or copies,

The robot Robotuna in its tank

the way a real bluefin tuna swims. They used the bluefin tuna as a model because it can swim so fast—about 40 miles per hour (64 kph). Like other fish, the bluefin tuna moves through the water by swinging its long, muscular tail from side to side. The first swing creates a large *vortex* (VAWR tehks), or whirlpool. The second swing creates a vortex that rotates in the opposite direction from the first one. When these two vortexes meet, they create a strong stream of water that pushes the fish forward.

Biomimesis
(By oh mih MEE sihs)
*is a new science that involves learning from animals. It comes from two Greek words—*bio, *meaning "life," and* mimesis, *meaning "imitation."*

A propeller on a submarine does the same thing, but not as efficiently as a fish's tail.

The tail also works as the fish's *rudder* (RUHD uhr). A rudder is the part of a boat that makes it turn. Actually, the fish's entire body moves to help it turn. A boat has a rudder for steering, but the *hull* (body) of the boat can't move the way a fish's body can. So the boat doesn't steer as efficiently and smoothly as the fish.

Ocean engineers are just beginning to learn how a fish's

body moves. Most fish have two *pectoral* (PEHK tuhr uhl) *fins,* one on each side of the front of the body. The pectoral fins control the diving rate of the fish, allowing it to go up and down in the water as it swims forward. These fins also control how the fish rolls from side to side, and they help the fish prepare for a turn. Submarines have similar structures called *diving planes.*

Ocean engineers have also discovered that fish use their pectoral fins and *ventral* (VEHN

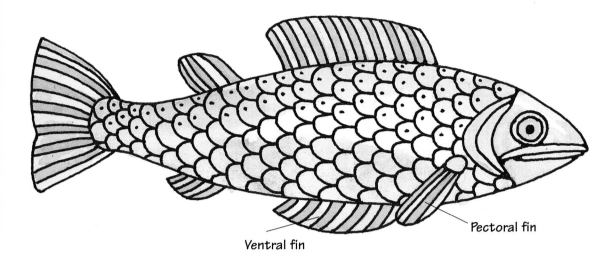

Pectoral fin

Ventral fin

truhl) *fins* for *hovering*—staying in one place in the water. *Ventral* means "belly," so it's no surprise that the ventral fins hang down from the fish's belly. By wiggling their pectoral and ventral fins ever so slightly, fish can make small movements backward or sideways when they are hovering. No one knows exactly how they do this.

When a fish or a ship moves through water, it meets an opposing force called *resistance.* A poorly designed ship needs a lot of energy to overcome resistance and begin to move. But a fish uses very little energy because its body is streamlined. A *streamlined* shape is rounded at the front and pointed behind. You may have seen streamlined bicycle helmets and cars. Submarines and other ships are also streamlined like fish.

When fish are swimming straight ahead, they do something that makes them even more streamlined. They fold their fins against their bodies. This action reduces *drag*—resistance caused by friction from the liquid around it. Ocean engineers who build small submarines are now thinking about making *retractable* diving planes. That means that the sub's "fins" could be pulled inside to reduce drag when the sub is simply gliding through the water.

As you can see, humans have learned quite a bit from studying fish, and we hope to learn even more.

Why does it take so much energy to paddle this raft? Because the raft isn't streamlined like a fish. The raft does not have a rounded front and a pointed behind to help it glide easily through the water.

How a Submarine Floats

Hmmmm . . . I wonder . . .
How does a submarine keep
from sinking to the bottom?
How does it rise to
the surface?

GATHER TOOLS

- two plastic 1-liter or
  2-liter soda bottles with
  screw caps

- a plastic straw or a 12-inch
  (30-cm) length of plastic
  tubing (You can get this
  from an aquarium store.)

- a small tub or sink full of
  water

Set up and give it a try

1 Fill a bottle to the very top with
water and cap it tightly. Now put the
bottle in the tub of water. What
happens?

2 While your bottle is still underwater, take the cap off. Put the straw in the bottle and slowly blow air into it. You will see bubbles rising and a pocket of air in the bottle—your breath is forcing water out of the bottle.

3 Cap the bottle and see what happens. Experiment to get the right amount of air and water inside the bottle so that it will float just beneath the surface of the water.

Try it again and again

- Fill the bottle with hot water.
- Fill the bottle with ice water, but leave out the ice cubes.

Set up a control

Put the cap on an empty bottle. Try to make the bottle stay underwater in your sink or tub. What happens?

Now, write it down

Jot down your observations from your lab. What makes the bottle float or sink? How can you explain this? How is your bottle like a submarine?

Compare your notes with those on page 32.

How a River Changes as It Flows

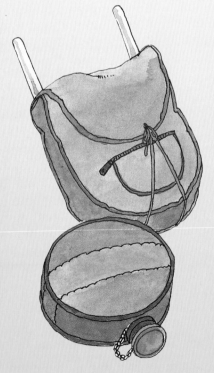

I'm Faye Delaponde. I'm a geographer—that means I study physical features on the surface of the earth. I specialize in the study of inland bodies of water such as lakes, ponds, and rivers. I'd like to introduce you to rivers first. People depend on rivers for drinking water, water for agriculture, and transportation.

The world is filled with important rivers—the Nile in Africa, the Amazon in South America, the Rhine in Europe, the Ganges in India, and many others. Rivers aren't all alike, but they do have some things in common.

Most big rivers start from a small source, such as a mountain *glacier* (mass of ice) or a spring. They follow gravity downhill. And sooner or later, all rivers flow into a body of water such as the sea.

Spring

Tributary

AHA!

The highest waterfall in the world is Angel Falls in Venezuela. It is 3,212 feet (979 m) high. The second highest is Mardalsfossen (Southern) Falls in Norway. It is 2,149 feet (655 m) high.

We'll start our journey near the top of a high mountainside, where a spring spurts out water. The water trickles downhill. Soon several tiny springs join together and form a larger stream. Rainwater adds to the river, too. This water runs downhill, carving out a bed as it goes and picking up speed.

As the rushing stream splashes and foams against rocks, it picks up oxygen from the air. This part of the stream is an oxygen-rich habitat for living things. But they have to swim fast or hold tight! That's why we find strong swimmers such as trout in this mountain stream. We'll also find flatworms, insect larvae, and tiny, plantlike algae (AL jee) clinging to the rocks.

Waterfalls usually occur in mountainous regions, and our growing stream has one. Up ahead the water flows over hard rock down to lower ground. Look at the waterfall plunging down the side of the cliff.

This river isn't done with rough play yet. I see rapids ahead. *Rapids* are a steep, narrow stretch of the river where water rushes very quickly over rocks or boulders. The fast-moving water creates bubbles and sometimes whitecaps.

Now that we're past the rapids, we can go rafting. Hop aboard.

All of the other streams that you see joining the river are called *tributaries* (TRIHB yuh TAYR eez). The river together with all of its tributaries is known as a *river system.* At the same time, *ground wate*r (water beneath the surface of the earth) seeps into the riverbed. The river grows larger.

Farther along, the land gradually flattens out. The river broadens

AHA!

The tambaqui (tahm BAH kee) is a fish that lives in the Amazon flood plain. It has huge, crushing teeth—more like a horse's than a fish's. These teeth allow it to eat tough fruits and seeds that fall into the water.

Waterfall

Rapids

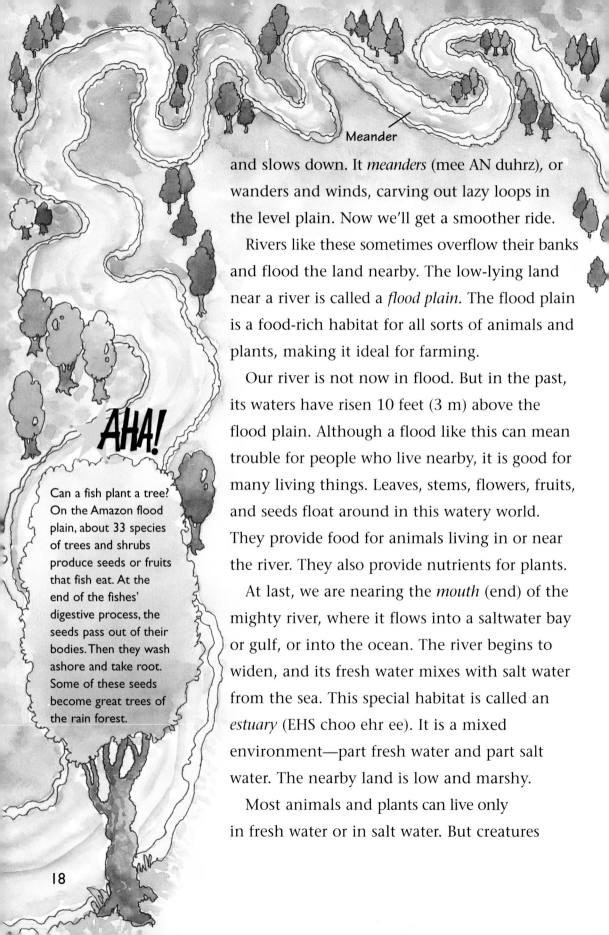

Meander

and slows down. It *meanders* (mee AN duhrz), or wanders and winds, carving out lazy loops in the level plain. Now we'll get a smoother ride.

Rivers like these sometimes overflow their banks and flood the land nearby. The low-lying land near a river is called a *flood plain.* The flood plain is a food-rich habitat for all sorts of animals and plants, making it ideal for farming.

Our river is not now in flood. But in the past, its waters have risen 10 feet (3 m) above the flood plain. Although a flood like this can mean trouble for people who live nearby, it is good for many living things. Leaves, stems, flowers, fruits, and seeds float around in this watery world. They provide food for animals living in or near the river. They also provide nutrients for plants.

At last, we are nearing the *mouth* (end) of the mighty river, where it flows into a saltwater bay or gulf, or into the ocean. The river begins to widen, and its fresh water mixes with salt water from the sea. This special habitat is called an *estuary* (EHS choo ehr ee). It is a mixed environment—part fresh water and part salt water. The nearby land is low and marshy.

Most animals and plants can live only in fresh water or in salt water. But creatures

AHA!

Can a fish plant a tree? On the Amazon flood plain, about 33 species of trees and shrubs produce seeds or fruits that fish eat. At the end of the fishes' digestive process, the seeds pass out of their bodies. Then they wash ashore and take root. Some of these seeds become great trees of the rain forest.

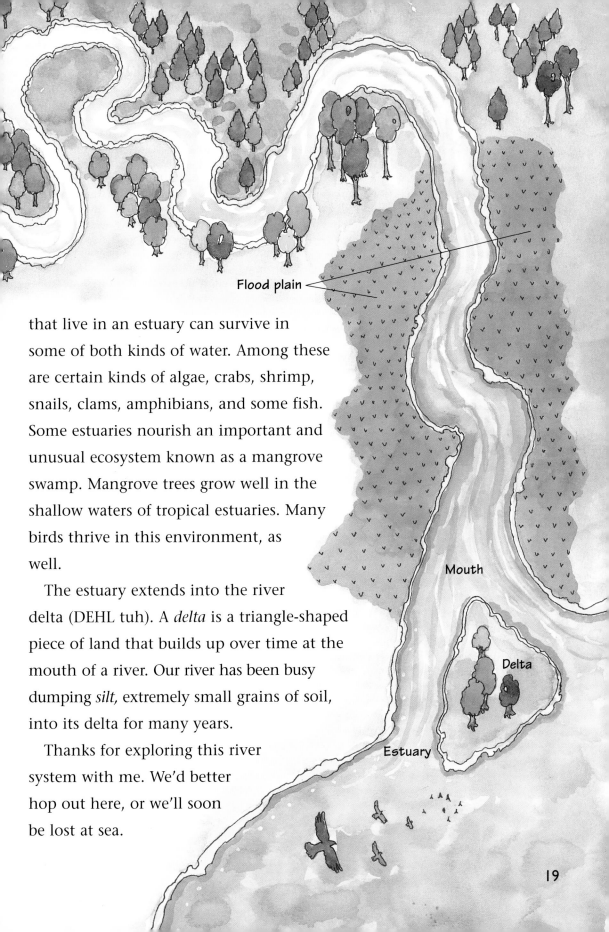

Flood plain

that live in an estuary can survive in
some of both kinds of water. Among these
are certain kinds of algae, crabs, shrimp,
snails, clams, amphibians, and some fish.
Some estuaries nourish an important and
unusual ecosystem known as a mangrove
swamp. Mangrove trees grow well in the
shallow waters of tropical estuaries. Many
birds thrive in this environment, as
well.

The estuary extends into the river
delta (DEHL tuh). A *delta* is a triangle-shaped
piece of land that builds up over time at the
mouth of a river. Our river has been busy
dumping *silt,* extremely small grains of soil,
into its delta for many years.

Thanks for exploring this river
system with me. We'd better
hop out here, or we'll soon
be lost at sea.

Mouth

Delta

Estuary

A Model River

Help these students label their science project—a model of a river system. Pair each label from the pile on the table with the proper letter label on the model. The answers are listed at the bottom of the next page.

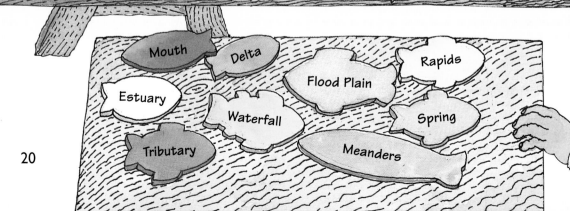

A. Meanders B. Mouth C. Estuary D. Tributary
E. Delta F. Waterfall G. Flood Plain H. Rapids I. Spring

Counting Creatures

If you want to know about the water quality of a river or stream, just ask an insect. Well, you can't *really* ask an insect, but you can find out how clean the water is by studying insects and other creatures affected by pollution.

An **environmental scientist** *studies the quality of land, air, and water as environments for living things. Environmental scientists are especially concerned with the effects of pollution.*

I'm Flo Brooks, and I'm an environmental scientist. Cleansing pollution from rivers and streams is my specialty. I work with environmental groups, governments, and communities. Together, we decide whether a river is in trouble. If the river is polluted, we work together to clean it up.

I train volunteers to help me. The volunteers check water quality by collecting insects and other small animals from rivers and streams. The mix of creatures tells us a great deal about the health of a stream. In scientific terms, we do *biological monitoring* to test water quality. That means we use living things rather than tests with chemicals to judge how healthy or polluted a body of water is.

How can we get so much information from these small animals? Please let me explain.

Many different kinds of insects lay their eggs in fresh water, and the larvae develop there. The larvae of the midge—a kind of small fly—and some other insects can stand more pollution than others. These are called *pollution-tolerant* animals. Larvae of other insects, such as stone flies, riffle beetles, and mayflies, are very sensitive to pollution. Pollution kills them. We call these insects *pollution-sensitive* creatures.

If we find a large number of pollution-sensitive insects in a stream or river, then we know the water quality must be good. But if we find only pollution-tolerant insects, that means trouble! Something has polluted the water and killed the pollution-sensitive critters.

Some animals, such as crayfish, dragonfly nymphs, and clams, are middle-of-the-roaders. They can live in water of just fair quality.

Students stir the stream bed to gather specimens from the bottom of the stream.

24

OK! Now that you understand the basic principles, I'll explain how we collect samples. Volunteers work in parts of a river that are shallow enough to wade in. Of course, we make sure they're properly dressed for this wet work. And every child is teamed up with an adult.

The volunteers use nets to collect specimens—insects or other living things—from the water. One type of net is called a *dip net.* It's just a net on the end of a long handle. It catches anything floating around in the water.

We use a *kick-seine* (kihk-sayn) net to collect samples from the stream bottom. The kick-seine is a mesh net—about 3 feet by 3 feet (1 m by 1 m)—strung between two poles. The volunteer kicks up material from the stream bottom, and it settles in the net. This kicking disturbs more creatures than we catch, but they quickly sink back down and carry on their activities. We also pick up rocks and rub them to collect creatures that cling with claws or suckers.

After collecting specimens in a net, students sort them.

The animals we get from the stream bottom help us check the river's oxygen content. Bottom-dwelling animals depend on oxygen that is dissolved in the water. If a good number of these creatures show up in our nets, we know the oxygen content is good. But if we collect very few bottom-living creatures, the oxygen content is probably poor.

The volunteers also identify insects. They carry a magnifying box, a plastic ice tray for sorting, and a "bug card" that has drawings of various river creatures.

Young volunteers play an important part in river monitoring. They have very good eyesight and excellent observation skills. Young children can learn to match a specimen with a picture on the bug card—even if they can't pronounce the critter's name.

Our volunteers do this collecting four to six times a year. And we always go back to the same places, or *testing stations*. Can you guess why?

You're probably wondering what happens at the end of all this testing. Well, environmental scientists like me study the data and draw conclusions about our subject— the river or stream. Then we make recommendations to the communities or governments concerned about water pollution.

A student uses a bug card to identify specimens.

This type of "bug testing" for water pollution works well all over the world. The same kinds of animals live in streams and rivers everywhere. For example, there are more than 400 species of mayflies worldwide, and you'll find at least one or two of them in any stream.

Oops, I'd better go! I've got some more bugs to count. See you soon. Maybe some day you'll be one of my volunteers.

Filtering Water

Hmmmm . . . I wonder . . .
What turns dirty water into
clean water?
How does a filter work?

GATHER TOOLS

- scissors
- absorbent cotton
- clean, small pebbles
- clean gravel
- clean sand
- water
- a small pitcher, such as a measuring pitcher
- a small cup or jar of soil
- two plastic bottles, each 17 ounces (1/2 liter)
- two jars or glasses

Set up and give it a try

1 Cut off the bottom of one of the plastic bottles with your scissors. (Ask an adult to help you.)

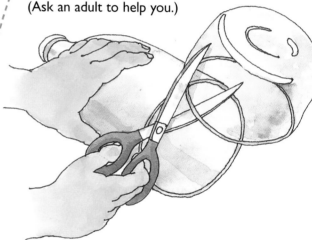

2 Tightly pack cotton into the neck of the bottle. Then turn the bottle upside down and put it in one of the jars. The bottle should stand straight and not touch the bottom of the jar.

3 In the bottle, put a layer of pebbles, then a layer of gravel, and finally sand. Use about 1/4 cup (60 ml) of each.

4 Pour 1 cup (240 ml) of water into the pitcher. Add two teaspoons (10 ml) of soil and stir well to make the water dirty.

Caution! Don't drink this water. Even though it may look clean, it still contains germs that could make you sick. A water-treatment plant adds germ-killing chemicals to the water.

5 Slowly pour dirty water into the bottle. If the filter layers seem to sink or mix together, the cotton may not be packed tightly enough. Pack more into the neck of the bottle. Let the water drain through.

Sand

Gravel

Pebbles

Cotton

Set up a control

To test the usefulness of a filter material—sand, gravel, or pebbles—make another filter without that material and compare your results.

Try it again and again

- Use thicker or thinner layers of the filter materials.
- Pour the water through the filter more than once.

Now, write it down

Jot down how the water looked just before you poured it through your filter. How did the water look after you filtered it? What did your filter take out of the water?

Compare your notes with those on page 32.

Why Rivers Curve This Way and That

(A Korean folk tale)

In a small town with a big pond there once lived a man named Yi Song-gye. He was a famous archer, but he also liked to fish. Every day he used to fish in the pond.

One day, while he was fishing, Yi Song-gye fell asleep. In a dream, he saw an old man with silvery-white hair.

"I am the owner of this pond," the man said, "but a dragon is trying to steal it from me. If you will kill the dragon, I will make you ruler of a kingdom."

"What a strange dream," Yi Song-gye thought when he woke. But as he watched, two dragons, one black and one yellow, rose from the pond. They were fighting furiously.

Yi Song-gye didn't know what to do. As he watched, the dragons sank again and disappeared.

The next day, when Yi Song-gye went fishing, he fell asleep again. Again the old man appeared in a dream. "Why didn't you kill the dragon?" he asked.

"I didn't know which one to kill," said Yi Song-gye.

"The black one," said the old man.

No sooner did Yi Song-gye wake than the dragons appeared again, lashing their tails and striking with their great claws. Yi Song-gye took his bow and shot the black dragon.

The yellow dragon swam away. The black dragon roared in pain and ran toward the sea, twisting and turning its great body. As it ran, it carved a river, and water began to flow from the pond down the twisting, turning path to the sea.

The dragon plunged into the ocean and died. From then on, rivers began to meander—turn this way and that.

The old man never appeared again, but he kept his promise. Yi Song-gye became the ruler of Korea.

Think Safety!

While science is fun, it's not exactly play. So it's time to talk safety. When you are doing experiments, always remember the rule, "Safety first" Help prevent accidents in the following ways:

- Before you begin a lab, read all instructions carefully. If you don't fully understand an instruction, ask a grown-up for help.

- Avoid spills, but just in case, line your work area with old newspapers before starting an experiment.

- While doing an experiment, do not eat or drink anything. Never, never put substances in your mouth.

- Keep first-aid supplies handy. Make sure you know where they are.

- If in doubt, don't do it. Taking chances can harm you or others.

- Ask a grown-up for help whenever you use chemicals, heat, sharp objects, or anything else that can hurt you.

- When you work with chemicals or flames, always wear safety goggles to protect your eyes.

- Don't fool around—it can be dangerous! Have fun, but treat your science experiments seriously.

Lab Notes

Here are some notes and findings you may have made when doing the labs presented in this book. There aren't any right or wrong notes. In fact, you probably made many observations different from the ones given here. That's okay. What can you conclude from them? If a lab didn't turn out the way you thought it would, that's okay too. Do you know why it didn't? If not, go back and find out. After doing a lab, did you come up with more questions, different from the ones you had when you started? If you did, good. Grab your journal and your science kit and start looking for more answers!

pages 12-13 *How a Submarine Floats*

The air-filled bottle floats to the surface. The water-filled bottle sinks. By blowing air into the sunken bottle, water is pushed out of it. The underwater level of the bottle can be controlled by adjusting the amount of air and water in it. Submarines control their depth in the water by controlling the amount of air and water in their ballast (BAL uhst) tanks.

pages 28-29 *Filtering Water*

Dirty water drips slowly through the layers of the home-made filter. When the water drips out of the bottom layer, it looks clearer and cleaner. The water looks different because the cotton and other materials in the neck of the jar remove some soil and plant material from the water. Purification plants use other materials and chemicals to make water even cleaner— clean enough to drink.